THE SNOW WATCHER

ALSO BY CHASE TWICHELL

Northern Spy (1981)

The Odds (1986)

Perdido (1991)

The Ghost of Eden (1995)

CHASE TWICHELL

THE SNOW WATCHER

Ontario Review Press, Princeton NJ

Ontario Review Press
9 Honey Brook Drive
Princeton, NJ 08540

Distributed by George Braziller, Inc.
171 Madison Avenue
New York, NY 10016

Library of Congress Cataloging-in-Publication Data

Twichell, Chase, 1950–
        The snow watcher / Chase Twichell.
                p.   cm.
        ISBN 0-86538-092-9
        ISBN 0-86538-093-7 (pbk.)
        I. Title.
PS3570.W47S66   1998
811'.54—dc21   98-20590
                                                          CIP

First Edition

ACKNOWLEDGMENTS

The book's title was taken from a one-line poem by an unknown nine-year-old: "I push through a crowd of snow watchers." Published in *Miracle Finger, a Book of Works by Children,* Salted Feathers, Portland, Oregon, 1975.

Cover image: mass-produced Japanese lithograph, date and artist unknown.

These poems owe a debt to traditional Japanese forms, particularly the tanka, and to the works of Eihei Dogen. The epigraph is taken from Dogen's "Genjo Koan," the first fascicle of *Shobogenzo,* a compilation of his life's work; translation by Robert Aiken, revised by Taizan Maezumi-Roshi and Francis Dojun Cook, in *Moon in a Dewdrop,* Kazuaki Tanahashi, editor, North Point Press, San Francisco, 1985.

The italicized lines in "The Voice of the Air" are Paul Eluard's. "Silver and White Elegy" is a riff on a passage in Ch'ing-yuan. Phrases in "Stirred up by Rain" and "Stray" were suggested by Thomas Cleary's translation of Muso Kokushi's *Dream Conversations,* Shambhala, Boston, 1996.

I'd like to express my gratitude to John Daido Loori, Abbot of Zen Mountain Monastery, for his teachings.

"Erotic Energy" is for Maia Banks, "Glimpse" for Arturo Patten, "Roach Holder, Circa 1967" for Heather McHugh, and "Cloud of Unknowing" for Mark Jarman. "The Horse-Angel" is an elegy for William Matthews.

Thank you, American Academy of Arts and Letters, for an award that gave me time to work on this book.

Thanks also to the editors of the following magazines, where poems were first published, sometimes in earlier forms:

AGNI: "Solo," "The Black Triangle," "Visitors." CRAB ORCHARD REVIEW: "White Pine." DENVER QUARTERLY: "Eleven Hours," "The Voice of the Air," "My Taste for Trash," "Hunger for Something," "Summer Rain." FENCE: "Girl Riding Bareback," "Bees." GRAFITTI RAG: "A Last Look Back," "If You Asked Me." GREEN MOUNTAINS REVIEW: "Walking Meditation," "My Skeleton," "Today's Lapses," 'The Mark," "For the Reader: Polaroids." THE IOWA REVIEW: "The Verge," "The Language of the Cloud," "Paint." THE KENYON REVIEW: "The Innocent One," "Private Airplane," "Saint Animal." THE KSHANTI REVIEW (web site): "Zazen, Wired & Tired," "Mountains and Rivers," "Cat and Mirror," "Weightless, Like a River," "Stray," "Tulip," "Disturbances of Thought." MID-AMERICAN REVIEW: "Stirred up by Rain." THE NEW YORKER: "Horse," "Road Tar." ONTARIO REVIEW: "Arsonist and Fireman," "Snow," "Silver and White Elegy," "Kerosene," "The Lost Birds," "Lilacs Again," "Locust." THE PARIS REVIEW: "Pine." PLOUGHSHARES: "Decade," "Tea Mind" (also on web site). SALMAGUNDI: "Kid Music," "Glimpse." SLATE (web site): "My Toshiba," "Roach Holder, Circa 1967." THIRD COAST: "Makeshifts," "The Wars," "Altars," "Animal Languages." WILLOW SPRINGS: "Little Yellow Flowers," "Mistake," "Minor Problems." THE YALE REVIEW: "Erotic Energy," "Secrets."

To R.B.

CONTENTS

To study the buddha way is to study the self. To study the self is to forget the self. To forget the self is to be actualized by myriad things. When actualized by myriad things, your body and mind as well as the bodies and minds of others drop away. No trace of realization remains, and this no-trace continues endlessly.

— Dogen

THE SNOW WATCHER

ROAD TAR

A kid said you could chew road tar
if you got it before it cooled,
black globule with a just-forming skin.
He said it was better than cigarettes.
He said he *had a taste for it.*

On the same road, a squirrel
was doing the Watusi to free itself
from its crushed hindquarters.
A man on a bicycle stomped on its head,
then wiped his shoe on the grass.

It was *autumn,* the adult word for fall.
In school we saw a film called *Reproduction.*
The little snake-father poked his head
into the slippery future,
and a girl with a burned tongue was conceived.

THE BLACK TRIANGLE

The eye in the dollar bill watched me
through a sharp little hole, a triangle
cut in the sky. It said, *Come on,*
let's pretend we're echoes,
let's pretend we're shadows.

When parents fight at dinner,
a child's mind knows where to go.
It stands behind itself and looks out
through the eyes behind the eyes,
like its own echo, or shadow.

From my bed I could hear the carnival's
music and crude microphones,
the shriek and grind of its rides.
The eye in the sky-hole could see
its phony green and orange stars.

I climbed down the drainpipe and walked
away through the damp grass of summer.
There were voices everywhere,
but far too far away to tell me anything,
under the green and orange stars.

THE LOST BIRDS

People said the silence was spooky—
you could hear a mouse
cracking seeds in heaven.

It happens some years—the birds
go away, and no one knows why.

Then the other birds come,
and for a time the woods
are full of the lost ones.

Why can't other people hear them,
when I can hear them?

THE WARS

The edge of the woods,
pine silence underfoot,
light split into shafts by the clouds.
Across the field, the house.
On the kitchen table,

the wine is already open,
the thin white plates laid out—
I can see their exact cold color,
the rare lamb sliced thin,
its blood still blood.

I've been out in the woods again,
half kid, half elder. A kid because
I'm waiting for the knives
of their voices to grow dull
so I can slip past them unarmed,

and an elder because I know
I'll never be weaponless again,
and soon I'll have to stand there,
a forged child, a kid-elder, among all
the dead soldiers of their two small armies.

KEROSENE

Here comes a new storm, roiling and black.
It's already raining up on Cascade,
where lightning makes the clouds look like

flowers of kerosene, like arson at the end
of the match. Lightning comes straight

from childhood, where the burned-out storms
still glitter weakly, tinsel on the dead trees
in the January streets. Back there a kid is still

learning why her parents need that harsh
backlight to see each other.

MISTAKE

It was as if someone had made a mistake,
as if the child had died but her ashes
went on falling softly through her life.

A bird came and lit on a snowy branch,
a purple finch still in its summer range,

come to celebrate the first winter
of the childhood by knocking a dust of stars
into the cold, so the baby could see the miracle.

I remember a window, a green curtain,
a bird in snow, then birdless snow.

PRIVATE AIRPLANE

On the grass airfield, a wife
is waiting in her four-wheel drive.
Soon her husband will appear
like a tiny black angel,
and when the winds and commotion

of his landing have come and gone
and I'm alone here again,
I'll carve a little memento of the evening—
a poem. As far back as I can remember,
this is how I've borne my attachment

to the world, trying to understand
what I am, scanning the sky for—what?
A god to tell me
why I'm the airplane,
and not its passenger?

GIRL RIDING BAREBACK

These late summer afternoons are so like childhood's
they take my breath and breathe it with me,
take it and breathe it without me.

Curved hot muscle of the neck, the chestnut shoulders
flowing through the uncut hay—

old August daydream come to visit
a place that looks familiar,
a field like the field it remembers—

arrows of sun falling harmless on a girl
and the big imaginary animal of her self.

GLIMPSE

It was as if a window suddenly blew open
and the sky outside the mind came flooding in.
My childhood shriveled to a close,

thread of smoke that rose
and touched a cloud—or the cloud's

replica adrift on the slow river of thinking—
and disappeared inside it. In that dark water,
a new lily was opening, sky-white out of the muck.

It was only a glimpse, quick,
like a bird ruffling,

but I saw the flower's
beautiful stark shape, an artichoke
brightened from within by the moon.

A path lay shadowy under my feet,
and I followed it.

LITTLE YELLOW FLOWERS

I don't know what they are,
fragile-looking but springy underfoot
so that I leave no tracks in them.
How did I overlook them?
They're everywhere.

I find them in Audubon: birdsfoot,
common. And yet I never saw them,
never touched their microscopic velvet
or shook a little of their pollen
onto the back of my hand to see the color.

On the high ledges above the house
the grasses grow up out of rock
into the scythe of the wind.
I want to wrap myself in that cloth—
air and the afterlife of plants.

Then the wind will be like a blind person,
unable to tell me from the grass,
me from the flowers
named for their seed pods,
which resemble the feet of birds.

CAT AND MIRROR

I'd like to turn my eyes
on the mirror's hard water
and not see myself,
not know myself to be me.
My young brown tiger-cat can do it—

he sniffs a little smear
where someone touched the glass,
happy to be on the bureau, so high up.
From there he can survey the entire
kingdom of the moment, and rule it.

THE YEAR I GOT RID OF
EVERYTHING

A huge invisible magnet dragged me
up into its powers. It lifted me high above
the beautiful wool carpets and the books.

I put on a dress made of bones
and danced alone in the great emptiness.

WEIGHTLESS, LIKE A RIVER

I heard of a teacher and went to meet him.
In the monastery I studied his words
and the way he moved his body.

He seemed weightless, like a river,
both in his words and in his body.

Dawn zazen, the windows'
river light... I heard
his bare feet on the wood floor.

All the slow fish of ignorance
turned toward the sound.

PINE

The first night at the monastery,
a moth lit on my sleeve by firelight,
long after the first frost.

A short stick of incense burns
thirty minutes, fresh thread of pine
rising through the old pine of the hours.

Summer is trapped under the thin
glass on the brook, making
the sound of an emptying bottle.

Before the long silence,
the monks make a long soft rustling,
adjusting their robes.

The deer are safe now. Their tracks
are made of snow. The wind has dragged
its branches over their history.

ZAZEN, WIRED & TIRED

It's like thrashing out past the breakers
into the opaque green swells,
the alien salt a thrill. The beach
is lightbulb-white, and sears
whoever lies down on it to rest.

An animal chooses this place
for its den and winters here,
sleeping month after month
in the musk of its own absence
so it can awaken more fully human.

Sitting zazen is like trying to be a tree.
I'm bad at it, impatient. I want the way
into the sap and wood to be violent, athletic,
so I keep my mind chopping at it, asking
how can I become the tree, if I am the tree?

IGNORANT POEM

I follow my breath as it goes in,
goes out. I want to know what I am—
a bellows of flesh, but what else?

That's what the stillness sings about,
day and night in the pine gloom.

The words of the sutra
call up all the new questions.
How can I be still in their presence?

The words are hanging fruits, too high
for even the tallest ladders of reason.

IMAGINARY DOKUSAN:
STRANGER

How suddenly you appeared,
like an animal in headlights–a teacher
who's already taught me what a poor
human spirit I am, a real beggar. Think of me,
wanting a simple stranger to be like a god.

ELEVEN HOURS

I sat all day in the quiet room,
clockless and unmoving, mind
roaming the unlit suburbs of the hours

where the self plays out
its vivid fictions—

a girl crouched in a yard, but she
wouldn't come back into words with me.
I had to leave her jangling

the chain link fence with her little arms,
her and the others I saw there—

the wife without child, the spirit
waking in the dark, thinking itself
purified by liturgy and robe—

I left them behind like beloved animals,
knowing the world would not shelter them.

SOLO

Nothing to watch but the snow,
the muted road slowly unbending.
I've always been alone, and that knowledge

has been like a sheet of cold glass
between me and the world,

though it meant I could
lose myself in lonely beauties,
for example the tiny

darting fish in the headlights,
their almost wordlike scribbling.

Now that's all changed.
I am myself nothing but a quick
flake of frozen cloud,

a minnow of light that can swim
silver-bodied into the questions,

the shadowy currents
of all I long to know.
That darkness without shores.

That's what I want to be. One fish
in the numberless fish of the snow.

ANIMAL LANGUAGES

In snow, all tracks
—animal and human—
speak to one another,

a long conversation that keeps breaking off
then starting up again.

I want to read those pages
instead of the kind
made of human words.

I want to write in the language of those
who have been to that place before me.

WILD MARE

A wild mare comes down out of the secret canyon
to drink the long shadows of the valley.
Not even the birds know her name,
which means suffering. Now she raises
her dripping muzzle and studies me.

ALTARS

Birch bark was paper and kindling, sandals
for the children of the trees, but because
it was sacred we rarely touched it.

A clean set of bear tracks,
mother and two cubs. Quick, rain—
erase them.

When the balsams give off
their silver glimpses, it means a god is coming
to teach us about thunder and bright tears.

August, month of my birth.
Skewered on two green sticks,
a little trout blackens in the fire.

The first few raspberries, in the hand of a man
who will later hurt me. The child,
feeding like a young bear on that fruit.

KID MUSIC

I aimed this arrow
at the music I loved
as a child, but instead

it pierced the child,
a girl of four or five who asks to sit

next to the family friend at dinner
and sing "Mack the Knife" for him,
her favorite song, in the busy kitchen.

She scares him under the table
with her hand, but she doesn't betray him.

She guards his secret devotions.
Why shouldn't she? She's his chosen one,
his brainy tomboy who already knows

the sound of the mind's waterfall endlessly
catching itself in a stone bowl

of its own making, a sound like applause
with silence in all its fissures,
or the sweeping sound of blowing snow,

intervals of pure silence in the ongoing hush.
She sings to send her voice like a moth

against the ceiling of the beautiful
empty room he has built for her,
where she can stay alone as long as she wants to

after he leaves, and listen to nothing,
the sound of whatever's happening—

the furnace kicking on,
red squirrels screeching in the pines,
the UPS man's radio.

What difference does it make?
All music calls up the first music.

LILACS AGAIN

A bridge of lilacs crosses the brook
that runs out of childhood,
as if childhood were a spring and not

a thirst. Cold water, fast water,
ache of that cold, remembering.

That quenching. An outdoor museum—
that's my childhood. Lilacs so thick
you can hear the bees from far away.

Thick with scent, thick with bees,
all drowned in the noise of the brook.

What did I mean, "a bridge of lilacs"?
That their branches touched each other
over the water? That their dark perfume

could take me back—take me
and never bring me back?

SECRETS

All my childhood was spent
in a clubhouse for one.
Who knows the password?

I'm still afraid of the subway.
What does it mean,
the sudden telling of a secret?

There was a pure light in childhood.
It was a laser. The girl stayed in the dark,
but the pure thing burned everything.

The light again. The word *pure.*
She lay on a dish-towel. Then with the same
fingers he played the piano.

Fold up the little towel
and put it away. Fold up
the little towel, put it away.

HOLOGRAM

At the center of the iris,
there's nothing.
You can look right into
its internal darkness
as into an unlit doll's house:

on the dining room table
a flower in a vase,
of course a tiny iris.
I'm peering in the window
of depression's house,

where I lived as a child.
It's like the inside
of an iris, twilit,
its innermost petals
closed softly over nothing.

ARSONIST AND FIREMAN

It was the hot orange edge,
the flame biting and tearing its way
out of the field–that's what I loved.

I looked up the word 'loins' in the dictionary,
and lit the dry grass with its meaning.

Put that memory away now. Its magnet
is weak after all these years. It's time to stop.
He's dead, long dead, dead for years.

Let his sad soul go off by itself.
Let it rest for a while in the scorched grass.

THE INNOCENT ONE

The watcher guarded the innocent one,
that was their relationship.
When the innocent one was in danger,

had angered the mother or the father
maybe, walked out on some thin ice

on purpose (for the sharp defining edges
of it) and suddenly needed a rescue,
the watcher would be the rescuer.

That allowed the innocent one to grow up
reckless: she was always stabbing herself

in the heart to see what each new kind of love
felt like. Then her savior the watcher
would heal her wound by explaining everything.

We're a very solid couple, the two of us.
We've grown up into a fine double person.

HORSE

I've never seen a soul detached from its gender,
but I'd like to. I'd like to see my own that way,
free of its female tethers. Maybe it would be like
riding a horse. The rider's the human one,
but everyone looks at the horse.

SAINT ANIMAL

Suddenly it was clear to me—
I was something I hadn't been before.
It was as if the animal part of my being

had reached some maturity that gave it
authority, and had begun to use it.

I thought about death for two years.
My animal flailed and tore at its cage
till I let it go. I watched it

drift out into the easy eddies of twilight
and then veer off, not knowing me.

I'm not a bird but I'm inhabited by a spirit
that's uplifting me. It's my animal, my saint
and soldier, my flame of yearning,

come back to tell me
what it was like to be without me.

DECADE

I had only one prayer, but it spread
like lilies, a single flower duplicating
itself over and over until it was rampant,

uncountable. At ten I lay dreaming
in its crushed green blades.

How did I come by it, strange notion
that the hard stems of rage could be broken,
that the lilies were made of words,

my words? Each one I picked
laid a wish to rest. I mean killed it.

The difference between prayer
and a wish is that a wish knows it will be
a failure even as it sets out,

whereas a prayer is still innocent.
Wishing wants prayer to find that out.

EROTIC ENERGY

Don't tell me we're not like plants,
sending out a shoot when we need to,
or spikes, poisonous oils, or flowers.

Come to me but only when I say,
that's how plants announce

the rules of propagation.
Even children know this. You can
see them imitating all the moves

with their bright plastic toys.
So that, years later, at the moment

the girl's body finally says yes
to the end of childhood,
a green pail with an orange shovel

will appear in her mind like a tropical
blossom she has never seen before.

A LAST LOOK BACK

Things change behind my back.
The starting snow I was just watching
has escaped into the past.

Well, not the past, but the part of the world
that surrounds the moment at hand.

That's why, whenever I see
animal tracks in a light snow like this,
I think of footnotes.

So strange, to inhabit a space
and then leave it vacant, standing open.

Each change in me is a stone step
beneath the blur of snow.
In spring the sharp edges cut through.

When I look back, I see my former selves,
numerous as the trees.

MAKESHIFTS

Nothing has a name it can't
slip out of. The waterfall is solid ice
by late November; the white pines
vanish under snow that's
blue in the morning, pink in the dusk.

Here's a little bouquet—ice
and evergreen and sun, three moments
arranged for human looking,
though it's only the husks of their names
that I've gathered and paralyzed.

IMAGINARY DOKUSAN: AUTUMN RAIN

This is the first rain of autumn,
something to which I always pay homage,
as I am now, through you.

It makes me sad and joyful, as if I were
the mother of the clouds it came from.

Is that emotion a phantom, too?
What is it that feels the wind at dawn,
and knows rain is coming?

I need a new word for the self,
and a new language in which to say it.

IMAGINARY DOKUSAN: BARKING DOG

The long tail of my history
no longer represents me.
It represents the various forms I took

in previous lives. Probably the being
speaking to you today will likewise disappear.

In the meantime, I hear a coy-dog
barking on the mountain. I bet he comes down
close to the monastery's lit windows to listen,

to smell the sleeping kitchen, its human food
abrupt against the thousand-scented woods.

When he's hungry, he eats, but he doesn't say
"thank you for putting food in my bowl."
His bowl is the wild woods.

How can I be like the dog? He's invisible.
He goes on barking, and doesn't imagine me.

SILVER AND WHITE ELEGY

It listens to me with its shadow ears,
brook that's no longer only water,
though someday it will be only water again.

I ask it, What part of you knows me?
Does human speech touch you in any way?

Maybe as a disturbance
the size of a small trout rising?
I hope I touch you,

because you have risen like that in me,
silver and white words, night after night.

Mirage of fields and sky. Grasses bending,
heavy with seed, in the coarsely woven rain.
Each moment says goodbye in its own way.

But that's a lie, that those moments
were actually here once,

and were not dreamed.
Goodbye is the only word I say.
It comes out like a dog's voice, proprietary.

Mine, its says. Mine, mine. Brook of shadows,
what will it be like for us, this severance?

When I look at you and see that you are
only water again, will I be water too, home at last
from the far-off provinces of the self?

Will my voice swim in your voice?
Who will I be, until I become you?

SNOW

Every day it snows an inch or two,
muting the music in the pines.
Old music.

Snow holds back the dawn—
an extra minute of lying here
while the self sleeps on.

Walking home after midnight,
two miles to go. The snow
is telling a story two miles long.

Dead trucks for sale in the yards.
New trucks plough the roads
of the dying towns.

If ever I flee to wilderness to die,
it will be to snow. Thus this snow
at bed time comforts me.

VISITORS

Red fox flashing through the pines,
I see your maleness when it
smacks my headlights.

Poor spikehorn, lashed to the roof rack
under an inch of new snow.
First horns, last horns.

A heron lands on a river rock,
the granite they use for gravestones.
Sharp names in the rough stones.

In spring, ten thousand scents.
The snake flees the scythe
into the uncut grass.

Two squirrels take a pinecone apart,
petal by rough petal. Their tails
say *fuck you!* to hunger.

THE VERGE

Inside language there was always
an inkling,
a dark vein branching,

bird-tracks in river sand spelling out
the fact of themselves,

asking me to come toward them
and scratch among them with a stick
all the secrets I could no longer keep,

until my words were nothing
but lovely anarchic bird-prints themselves.

I think that's the verge right there,
where the two languages
intertwine, twigs and thorns,

words telling secrets
to no one but river and rain.

THE VOICE OF THE AIR

There's something I know
that no one taught me.
A voice in the air said it,

and the trees passed it among them.
I carry the words in my mind as if

they've always been there,
secret lullaby
sung by the clouds at night:

There is another world,
but it is in this one.

I've wasted this knowledge,
wasted it delighting in the musical
collusion of wind and leaves,

when wind in bare branches
was the sound I heard and believed.

I climb up onto the granite ledges
through the hard November woods
to hear its bone-song.

It's the voice of the air, and it tells me
I'll die in whichever world I choose.

MOUNTAINS AND RIVERS

Dry Waterfall—that's what it's called
in the language of the garden,
rocks and plants suggesting

a quick-running stream,
though it's only the eye that moves.

I just kept levering and nudging
rocks around until the place looked
a little trampled but serene.

Now last year's gray-blond grasses
flow over the granite's harsh striations,

which are also flowing.
Feet bare, I sweep the stone path,
two years old beneath an inch of leaves,

its half-buried cold reminding
my foot soles that each stone's

mostly underground,
still a part of the mountain.
I can see a little way

into the mystery of the lichens,
and they into mine.

My eyes flow over them
and vanish in the grass river,
which pours itself into the wind.

Acorns lie pink and splitting
among the first greening things,

but it's the big stones underfoot
that I love most as I squat to pick
a few damp leaves out of the moss,

because they have forgotten
the crowbar, as I have not.

WALKING MEDITATION

I'm the first tall animal
to walk the trail today.
Apologies to the spiders.

The sapling maple I cut
last year for a walking stick
forgives me this morning.

Galaxies of lichens
on the stones—what's
my life to them?

What do the deer
make of my trail? Sometimes
they use it, sometimes they don't.

The wind is a poor net.
The universe
swims right through it.

TEA MIND

Even as a child I could
induce it at will.
I'd go to where the big rocks

stayed cold in the woods all summer,
and tea mind would come to me

like water over stones, pool to pool,
and in that way I taught myself to think.
Green teas are my favorites, especially

the basket-fired Japanese ones
that smell of baled hay.

Thank you, makers of this tea.
Because of you my mind is still tonight,
transparent, a leaf in air.

Now it rides a subtle current.
Now it can finally disappear.

PAINT

Lotions and scents, ripe figs,
raw silk, the cat's striped pelt...
Fat marbles the universe.

I want to be a faint pencil line
under the important words,
the ones that tell the truth.

Delicious, the animal trace
of the brush in the paint,
crushed caviar of molecules.

A shadow comes to me and says,
When you go, please leave
the leafless branch unlocked.

I paint the goat's yellow eye,
and the latch on truth's door.
Open, eye and door.

MY TOSHIBA

Under the lake's black ice,
the largest trout not yet caught
fins in diluted moonlight.

My mind feels split in two—
one screen dark, one lit.
The dark one can't sleep.

Even when together,
some lovers
long for one another.

I'm tracking the animal
that leaves these
splayed prints in the snow.

Little sky of the mind.
A bird flies across
and leaves no trace.

HUNGER FOR SOMETHING

Sometimes I long to be the woodpile,
cut-apart trees soon to be smoke,
or even the smoke itself,

sinewy ghost of ash and air, going
wherever I want to, at least for a while.

Neither inside nor out,
neither lost nor home, no longer
a shape or a name, I'd pass through

all the broken windows of the world.
It's not a wish for consciousness to end.

It's not the appetite an army has
for its own emptying heart,
but a hunger to stand now and then

alone on the death-grounds,
where the dogs of the self are feeding.

DISTURBANCES OF THOUGHT

I step into a slim green boat
and its rope slithers into the lake.
Suddenly I'm free of what I know.

The boat is green for the spruces
of innocence from which it was cut.

I could lie, and say I've seen
a glimpse of what's inside the darkness,
that my feet already taste

the cold stones of the path,
but it's only the feet I know about.

Here I am, in a monastery
sitting in human silence.
How loud it is, and how surrounding,

bell before dawn in the stone building,
all the concentric silences.

No one is here with me.
Too late for good-byes, then.
On the altar of today I light

one candle for recklessness,
another for stamina.

MY SKELETON

My skeleton wants to eat nothing
but brown rice and water,
a few wild greens for energy.

It would like to live here
in the monastery and be called

"Hungry Ghost" in Japanese,
float through the zendo in robes
the color of itself.

Once, watching a snow squall
move down the valley,

a part of me lurched forward
as if to go meet it. It was my skeleton
imagining itself a long white ladder

to the clouds of snow. You can tell
a lot about the dreamer from the dream.

IMAGINARY DOKUSAN:
RAT

An emotion can start out hopeful
and end up with a knife sticking out of it,
yet it's one emotion.

I could be a spirit transforming itself.
Or I could be kneeling here undercover,

Ms. Zen taking secret notes for a poem,
about to slouch back into all her bad habits.
Every moment breaks open

into another possible life. Tonight,
this anxiety slinks across my mind like a rat.

MY TASTE FOR TRASH

I've got a taste for trashy thrillers,
their psychological sex and violence,
sometimes two in a night.

They're like heavy velvet curtains:
no stray light spoils the darkness,

no sound of the world comes through.
The real is elsewhere.
The real guns, cold to the touch.

The real boys, their eyes opaque,
no longer human.

And when they die,
they turn to stars in the star-clogged night.
This is a tale you could tell

any place on earth, in any century,
and people would already know it.

ROACH HOLDER, CIRCA 1967

Look what I have in my hand:
a slender silver tweezer
blackened by thirty years.

I still feel the ground under my back,
the heat of the little red star.

But now I'm old enough to tell my friend
about those days of growing-pain
in a way that makes her laugh.

I wished for a love that would take me
from my parents' house, and I got it.

Later I wished that that love
had not done me so much damage.
Why then have I saved its artifact?

Diminutive stab of grief.
Strange keepsake.

PASSING CLOUDS

One sip of self-understanding
and I'm drunk as the wind slurring
its words on the field.

Once in a while the cloud bank splits,
and I glimpse the perfect sky,
there all the time behind the mind's cumulus.

Like all intoxicants, self-knowledge
darkens the mind. It's a good thing surprise still
pierces that darkness with its white shoots.

When I cut the young maples,
light ploughed a garden in the field.
Now my stakes and string claim a square of shade.

The apples lie where they fall, hard and green
until the animals come to feed on them,
or the hungry frost.

SUMMER RAIN

First association: two sounds–
drops on the tent-fly,
spits of water in the fire.

Rain strips bare the soul's loneliness.
It kisses and touches it, then leaves it
alone to think about its enemies.

Animals don't pay much attention to rain.
Birds shelter themselves,
but mostly the animals just go on eating.

Rain is a lesson. It shows how
all things intermingle, how they
caress and yet devour each other.

Now think of this rain I've made for you.
Listener, how did you come to trust
I would not kiss and touch, then lie to you?

TO THE READER:
THE LANGUAGE OF THE CLOUD

Come with me to a private room.
I have a secret to show you.
Sometimes I like to stand outside it

with a stranger because I haven't
come at it from that vantage in so long—

see? There I am beside him, still joined,
still kissing. Isn't it dreamlike,
the way the bed drifts in its dishevelment?

Bereft of their clothes, two humans
lie entangled in its cloud.

Their bodies are saying the after-grace,
still dreaming in the language of the cloud.
Look at them, neither two nor one.

I want them to tell me what they know
before the amnesia takes them.

TODAY'S LAPSES

There's a country I like to visit.
We're like a man and his mistress—
I'm not going to marry it, not going to give it up.

I visit all three of its Provinces.
Their names are Anger, Ignorance, and Greed.

When I cross the line between embellishment
and a lie, there's a warning ache,
but also a scrap of color where none was.

Tomorrow, I'll spend some time pondering
the kinship of the color and the ache.

No zazen today. I've strayed off
on my own beyond the pasture's edge,
where the lupine's in full bloom.

Summer has just finished opening.
Don't look for me tonight.

MINOR PROBLEMS

This morning it seems likely
that my aspiration—to shed all my skins—
will end in one long papery
exhalation of relief at having asked myself
Why do this, anyway? For some other paradise?

Even the dark windows seem to attend
to the zendo's distinct layers of silence,
which I think of as a river with many currents.
When I look again, dawn has come closer,
no warmth in it at all.

I keep forgetting what it is
I've recently come to believe.
It transformed me, but now it
vanishes like a drug from my cells
and I'm a gray drifter again.

Various thoughts batter the one window,
big moths in moonlight.
They don't want to be my prisoners any more.
Have I thought these thoughts before,
but don't remember them?

I'm afraid of the infinite stairs,
of the mind that goes on talking
like a cut-off snake's head but doesn't stop
at sundown. It climbs
its own steep facade and falls back.

STRAY

The cat was starving, missing a foreleg,
and winter right next door.
A neighbor killed its pain with one shot.

My mind follows the delicate three-blossom tracks
across snow.

It won't leave the cat alone,
circling and circling the stiffening body
already claimed by the snow—

and I, the observer, follow it
as if I held its long unbreakable leash.

Look at the wind, invisible river,
look at the breaking mirror of the brook.
Is this the place where thoughts arise and vanish?

Which part is the cat,
and which the mind?

CLOUD OF UNKNOWING

In spring, the apple and cherry trees are clouds
in twenty shades of pink. Yet always,
behind them, a vaster radiance flares.
What I see, I see through drifts and veils—
there must be cloud in me too.

Snow is a cloud of distracting beauty,
its tiny sharp flowers aloft with weight
they can't bear. Each question must have a body.
I know my body, so what is my question?
Who speaks to me out of the blossoming cloud?

STIRRED UP BY RAIN

I fired up the mower
although it was about to rain—
a chill late September afternoon,
wild flowers re-seeding themselves
in the blue smoke of the gas-oil mix.

To be attached to things is illusion,
yet I'm attached to things.
Cold, clouds, wind, color—the sky
is what the brush-cutter wants to cut,
but again the sky is spared.

One of two things can happen:
either the noisy machine dissolves in the dusk
and the dusk takes refuge in the steady rain,
or the meadow wakes shorn of its flowers.
Believing is different than understanding.

THE HORSE-ANGEL

Outside the hotels along the park,
on the shore of the river of cars,

the horses stand in their harnesses.
Their bony shoulders make them look
fledgling, unfinished,

especially the little chestnut mare,
shivery and tense,

hiding her beautiful wings.
The streetlight drops a yellow cone
around her, to protect her,

but she draws my eye inside it
to where the wings stay furled.

BEES

The best berries are the last to ripen—
you can taste fall in them,
dark sugars that narcotize the wasps.

There's a long sting of attraction
in the way the brambles won't let go,
and in how I tear myself free.

The dog
yelps and rolls.
Ground bees.

Stop needling me, guilt.
If X is what's familiar,
then you minus X equals nothing.

The upside-down wine glass
warps and enlarges
the yellow jacket inside.

TO THE READER:
POLAROIDS

Who are you, austere little cloud
drawn to this page, this sky in the dream
I'm having of meeting you here?

There should be a word that means "tiny sky."
Probably there is, in Japanese.
A verbal Polaroid of a Polaroid.

But you're the sky, not a cloud.
I'm the cloud. I gather and dissipate,
but you are always here.

Leave a message for me if you can.
Break a twig on the lilac, or toss
a few dried petals on the hood of my car.

May neither of us forsake the other.
The cloud persists in the darkness,
but the darkness does not persist.

ARCHITECTURE

I peer into Japanese characters
as into faraway buildings
cut from the mind's trees.

In the late afternoon a small bird
shakes a branch, lets drop a white splash.

In the wind, in the rain,
the delicate wire cage glistens,
empty of suet.

Poetry's not window-cleaning.
It breaks the glass.

VIOLENCE TO LANGUAGE

There's a trail near here
called the Shorey Shortcut, one of those
affectionate but proprietary WASP coinages,

effectively a brand on property.
I came to a sign on the trail which said

"shortest route" next to a left-pointing arrow.
I chose that way, the more athletic route,
and this is part of it, these potholes,

this violence to language, elimination
of all the old elegances, one by one.

IMAGINARY DOKUSAN:
THISTLE

This evening the thistles' surprising blue
pierced the twilight.

I picked one spike-head, still closed,
and studied it. I know of no other
human experience like this one:

the self as a fistful of nails
longing to scatter in deep grass, to rust.

Three years I've spent,
chasing the shadow of the tree
away from the tree,

stalking invisible
deer in the moonlight,

afraid of coming face to face
with their antlers which might
blind me or throw me back at myself.

IMAGINARY DOKUSAN: PERFUME

Crushed lime halves in the sink,
a wood match's sweet-acrid strike...

I keep looking for things with a beauty
that's not incidental, but have found none.
Because of this, the difference between sensuality

and being fully awake in the moment
is often unclear to me, for example

the sun's smell of ripening
even in things still immature—
which of the two pleasures is that?

IMAGINARY DOKUSAN: FURNACE

Anger wears the rubies of the coals,
charred silk of the ash.

But ash isn't a translation of fire,
is it.
Fire stays fire.

INK STONE

It's a green river stone,
without adornment
except for a single
twig of pine
in an empty pool.

I like to scramble up the hill
in the summer dusk,
sit on a long stone left by the ice,
and watch the sky go dark
in a puddle of yesterday's rain.

STONE STEPS

Three stone steps lead
to where a granite outcrop
shelters a scrap of ledge,
the place I go to study
the shadow dust
spilled by the ferns,
the sky's old chandeliers.
I stand looking south
down the Keene Valley,
then inward,
toward the altar of the wall.
Above, day and night,
a small bell
that never rings dips
and rises on its supple branch.
My work is to know
what I am.

ICICLE

Snow fills the space
between me
and the mountain.

Inattentive,
my mind wanders
into its delicate flux.

I overhear myself
laughing. The snow and I—
one transience!

MYSTERY

Snow drags yards
of sequins over the road.
I hear its reptilian swishing,
an icy otherness
that speaks to me alone.

I always knew about
the other world,
that there was one,
that I would find
the way there.

In the hotel, a pool of lilies.
Only one flower:
a miniature lotus, gold.
I follow the child bride
wherever she goes.

If you do not see the way,
you do not see it
even as you walk on it,
wrote Master Shih-t'ou
in the eighth century.

It only seems
that each moment
begins green and closed,
and ends split open,
emptied of golden seed.

TULIP

It's slippery on the high fence
between self and moment.
Which side is which?
If the fence knows,
it's not telling.

Look, a yellow tulip
in the charcoal sky—
a vividness passing so quickly
I have to abandon the poem
to follow it.

WHITE PINE

Trees have been witness
to my life, have been emblem.
I've wept my griefs
into the high darkness
of their arms, cheek against
a cone's rough open scales.
The seeds that took
in my year, 1950,
have grown a foot a year.
My eye walks out
along a branch shining
in rain, and looks back
from a long way away.
In the twilight,
night's shadow means sleep,
and no one wants to.
We all want to stay out
playing kick-the-can,
wild for another half hour
with some new kids.

TO THE READER:
BLUNT ELEGY

I'm leaving now, closing
the cabinet of miniature clocks.
I want a clean goodbye
to the town of small towers
I built, now on the horizon,
and to you, temporary friend,
who remain unknown to me
as the face of the snow.

TO THE READER:
IF YOU ASKED ME

I want you with me, and yet you are the end
of my privacy. Do you see how these rooms
have become public? How we glance to see if–
who? Who did you imagine?
Surely we're not here alone, you and I.

I've been wandering
where the cold tracks of language
collapse into cinders, unburnable trash.
Beyond that, all I can see is the remote cold
of meteors before their avalanches of farewell.

If you asked me what words
a voice like this one says in parting,
I'd say, *I'm sweeping an empty factory*
toward which I feel neither hostility nor nostalgia.
I'm just a broom, sweeping.

TO THE READER:
TWILIGHT

Whenever I look
out at the snowy
mountains at this hour
and speak directly
into the ear of the sky,
it's you I'm thinking of.
You're like the spirits
the children invent
to inhabit the stuffed horse
and the doll.
I don't know who hears me.
I don't know who speaks
when the horse speaks.

NOTES

Eihei Dogen (1200--1253) was the Japanese Zen master who brought the Soto Buddhist teachings from China to Japan. He is revered not only as a profound and original religious thinker, but for the directness and immediacy of his written expression of the inner life.

Zazen is a form of seated meditation. Thought to be the most direct means to enlightenment, its purpose is to observe and ultimately to still the habitual activity of what we call the "self" so that we can perceive its true nature.

Dokusan is a private interview with the teacher, in which the student demonstrates his changing consciousness and receives guidance. Formal and highly ritualized, these exchanges between teacher and student are also unpredictable and intimate. All of the "Imaginary Dokusan" poems are addressed to the teacher.

The Cloud of Unknowing (anonymous, 14th century, exact date unknown) was probably written by an English clergyman. The book proposes a method of contemplation that analyzes and disables the intellect's resistance to what it cannot imagine.